M000041357

OPEN YOUR HEART TO LOVE

BY PREM SADASIVANANDA

Dedication

OM OM OM
Om Gam Ganapataye Namah
Om Namo Bhavagate Sivanandaya
Om Namo Bhagavate Vishnu-devanandaya

With these introductory mantras I make this offering to all in the form of this book on Love.

We all need inspirational words, the words that urge us to explore life and deepen our understanding of who we are. The spirit arouses, the words come and books thus happen!

It so happened that the creation of this book took place at the encouragement of a dear friend of mine, Maria Righini, who after having seen the inspirational posts I was putting on Facebook, suggested that I should compile them in the form of a book.

We all contemplate life and often wish to find a way to express the realizations we've had, and what we feel in the depths of our hearts and minds. These contemplations often carry a deeper knowledge, wisdom to whose voice we must learn to listen and live according to.

One of my favorite contemplations is that on the nature of Love. Love—often misunderstood as being only an emotion—transcends all definitions. It is spiritual by nature and it is the very expression of who we truly are. Love transcends all forms, names, languages, races, and peoples and rests in Her own domain, that of Spirit or Consciousness.

Love is the language of Heart and Oneness. All divisions and separation are insults to Her. Infinite are Her expressions of Love: kindness, sympathy, compassion, service, giving and charity, to name only a few. Love smiles, heals, and rejuvenates.

The inspiration behind my work has always been the wonderful spiritual writings of the great Master Sivananda whose words are forever etched in my heart and whose guidance I receive daily.

The purpose of this book will be accomplished if a word or a sentence from it inspires you to love and serve others.

Prem Sadasivananda

Acknowledgments

This book would have not taken birth without the grace of my guru Swami Vishnu-devananda whose silent presence and inspiration continue to fill every day of my life with love for service, yoga and knowledge.

My special gratitude goes to Maria do Carmo Righini for her encouragement to write this book.
To Maria's daughter Johanna Gyarfas, an incredibly talented artist for providing the beautiful drawings for the book.
To that wonderful spirit Dawn Bossman (Bharati) for the editorial work and her great patience!
To Ania Sluchak (Purna Devi), my old-time friend for her beautiful eye and masterly design.
To Stacey Antine (Devika) for her ongoing support and love.

And to all of my students and teachers from around the world whose friendship and love have contributed to the deepening of my knowledge.

OPEN YOUR HEART TO LOVE
copyright © 2015 by Prem Sadasivananda

All rights reserved. Printed in the USA by Vidyā-samyogah.

No part of this book may be used or reproduced in any manner
whatsoever without written permission from the publisher except in
the case of brief quotations embodied in critical articles and reviews.

For information, please visit **www.vidya-samyogah.com**.

Cover and layout design by Ania Sluchak (Purna Devi)
Illustrations by Johanna Gyarfas

ISBN: 978-1-68222-881-4

TABLE OF CONTENTS

"To live is to love. To love is to live.
You live that you may learn to love.
You love that you may learn to live in the Eternal.
In every inch of His creation, you can verily understand His
love. Love is joy. Love is warmth. Love is the golden tie which
binds heart to heart, soul to soul."

Sivananda

To Live Is To Love

The Power of Love

Love is the very nature of who we are as spiritual beings. The great prophets and sages said that the very Creation is born out of the love of the Supreme. We all carry the same God-consciousness within us and, therefore, the same seed of love. No one can suppress the urge for love.

Love is simply the recognition of our true nature or our essence (as Pure Consciousness) in another being. Because of its irresistibly attractive nature, consciously or unconsciously we all try to unite with all things, all beings.

True Love Needs Courage

To love is to assert the presence of the omnipotent Being that dwells within us. Leading a spiritual life is the same as embodying love. Love is the most natural spiritual practice.

Love means acceptance; accepting others as they are as they strive to be free from their weaknesses, limitations and fears.

Thus Love requires courage, and letting go of our own fears. Fear arises due to the feeling of separation from others— the feeling that there is something outside of 'me'. Fear is what separates us from others—it is the wall between the 'other' and us.

In true love you have nothing to lose, but only to gain. It is the only and the most certain method of self-healing, the healing of the whole of our being.

Whenever we reject or dislike somebody, however insignificant the reason for it may seem, we have, in fact, rejected a part of ourselves since we are in reality one with all.

Pure Love

Have you ever thought: 'What creates the distance between ourselves and others?'

The greater the identification with our self-image and the more we are preoccupied with our own preferences and notions, the greater the psychic distance between ourselves and others. Consequently we are less able to feel for and empathize with them. The limit thus set by one's own ego-identification acts as an impediment to the expansion needed to love others. Thus in order to be able to truly love we need to break free from the self-imprisonment created by our own mind.

Pure love breaks the boundaries of such limited self-definition and seeks to welcome all with her open arms.

From the crystal-like space in the heart, consisting of pure Light, love floods out to embrace all, especially the suffering and the needy. The practice of pure love is capable of bringing the whole Creation within its vast domain.

The Need for Love

Love alone is the true building material of our progress, and ultimately our enlightenment or liberation. Love is healing, redeeming, rejuvenating and liberating. It is the only thing needed. Love removes all differences and misunderstandings and heals the pain of being in this body.

Use love with confidence. Express it more and more.

Apply love and kindness as you are working with your own mind. Love is the light that nurtures the seed of our wisdom and compassion. Love as a tool of transformation is so frequently and painfully forgotten.

Love is to be lived moment by moment.

Loving All

"Love, embracing all beings, be they noble-minded or low-minded, good or evil. The noble and the good are embraced because love is flowing in them spontaneously. The low-minded and the evil-minded are included because they are those who are most in need of love. In many of them the seed of goodness may have died merely because warmth was lacking for its growth, because it perished from cold in a loveless world. Love, embracing all beings, knowing well that we all are fellow wayfarers through this round of existence - that we all are overcome by the same law of suffering." —Buddha

To love even those who are difficult to comprehend, accept or love because of their negative nature or deeds is what Jesus, Buddha and Swami Sivananda taught by their example. In the highest sense we are united spiritually but in this world we are united with no exception, by suffering in one form of another. The only healing balm is love.

In Gratitude to Love

We learn things by example, by emulation or by imitation. Our deepest notions, beliefs and understanding, our most profound thoughts and sentiments about love exist in their full blossom in our hearts only because we were influenced by or we learned about it from someone we deeply admired and loved.

The living symbol of love is the highest of all symbols. Such a symbol is nothing but the Heart of the Divine. There have always been living embodiments of true love. They are either the great masters of the science of spirituality, or the people who we knew were nothing but 'love'. There have been people in each of our lives who spoke, thought and acted only the language of love. They may have been in our life only for a few minutes, hours or days and yet the impact of their ability to love has forever been etched in our memory. Remember them today with gratitude and let the memory ring like a bell reminding you that, "All we need is (to learn and to give) love".

True Knowledge of Love

Only deeply aware people know love in its fullness and its essence. These kinds of people we call saints and sages. They are beacons of light for the whole of humanity and they set the standards for service and love. Usually the knowledge of love does not come to anybody without that person having suffered deeply.

This suffering is the Lord's or nature's way of breaking up the artificial boundaries created by our little self, or ego, and it is necessary in order for us to open our hearts. Suffering is a mystical key given to us to open the doors to the mysteries of creation and our inter-connectedness with all. Once we have gone through the fire of self-purification by giving of ourselves to others, our heart is ready to receive all. It is self-absorption or exaggerated self-concern that prevents us from feeling the inner world and the spirit of another person.

Learning From Great Masters

Even though we learn by instruction, we learn so much more by example. We may learn all possible words about how to love and yet not be able to bring it to life, but having a living, embodied example of love and kindness in our life leaves an indelible trace in our consciousness and spurs us into wanting to awaken the same love in our heart, and to give it to others.

Love includes self-sacrifice, self-offering and self-forgetfulness. When we read about, or see, or are around somebody who is so highly evolved as to make his or her life into an offering of love, we become highly inspired by his or her example, and want to follow in his or her steps.

Such is the power of those who are the great lovers of the Lord's creation that their very touch or look, or a word or act has transformed many and taught them the most important lesson in life—that of unconditional love!

Life's Lessons

The more we understand the traps of our own personality and the more we can fathom the meaning of the loud voice of the little 'I' (ego) within, the larger our heart becomes. Human suffering has a hidden meaning behind its appearance.

Whenever and wherever there may be a frozen space within us that no longer feels alive, where we become un-reactive and unresponsive to the larger life around us, to the presence of others and their lives, including the lives of plants and bushes, the sky above us, the lovely Mother Earth that holds us all in Her lap—in short, all nature—when in our lost sensitivity we feel either self-important or perhaps lonely and abandoned, the suffering comes to our rescue and melts all the rock-like crust of our illusion, breaking the walls between us and everything else, and opens the space for the rivers of life to rush in.

And then we start to feel love!

Fearless Love

Love proceeds only from the natural, original state of Being. It thrives on naturalness. It does not compromise itself with artificiality. It looks for the 'real' us and the 'real' in us. When we see the 'real' person in front of us, then love and respect will naturally be there.

It is this quality of 'Being-ness' that we share with the whole Creation, and it is from this Being-ness alone that attraction manifests and upon which love builds. Being-ness is the common meeting place of all love. Its dwelling place is the heart. There is a great attractiveness in simply being oneself.

Observe nature and you will see its innate beauty arising from Her artless simplicity of being. Babies, children, birds, animals, flowers, and simple, humble people—they all effortlessly display their naturalness, uniqueness, and their own beauty. They have nothing to add to or subtract from what they are. They are lovely just as they are. They are faithful to their own nature.

Modern civilization is built on the relinquishment of naturalness. Every form of human existence, from food to clothing and looks of people, to their manner of talking and looking, had to be modified away from their natural simplicity.

When you look at a person, what do you see? Often you may see their new hairstyle or clothing, their upbringing, their diplomas and achievements, but you cannot see them! They are serious, uptight, and proper, and do their best to hide what they feel, their vulnerability, their humor and naturalness, their humanness. They have built layers of artificial values into their personality. (Persona comes from Latin and it means 'a mask'.)

Fear is the foundation of much of our modern life. Love cannot thrive in a barren land. Humans must change in order to rediscover love. And if they let go of a need to be something or someone else rather than themselves, they will discover love everywhere, in every inch of creation. Such is the power of fearless love that it finds its reflection in all it meets.

Life as a Teacher

Love is the very reason we were born—to learn, to master, to perfect love. We have been given this life as a gift in order to master all forms of love and attain the Union with all elements, plants, animals, humans and the vast nature. The way love is learned is at times mysterious as it seems that we have been made to suffer in some way in order to open up like a flower or a seed.

In order to have our love perfected we may have had to be abandoned, betrayed, or wronged in some way so that we could suffer and thus learn forgiveness, patience, mercy and loving-tenderness. Whenever a need for a particular lesson or mastery has arisen in our nature, the forces of the whole Creation start to work together to provide us with a particular experience in order to begin our learning or growth. This is especially true when a part of us has become misaligned with the Creation, and some coldness has set in our hearts, and we have lost touch with our feelings.

Life is a mystery and nobody can ever know or calculate correctly what exact thing is needed in order for us to learn at any given time. To love is to invite the whole Creation into our life. Love is the spiritual force behind our evolution. It is the very backdrop of all experiences and the only path.

"You can search throughout the entire universe for someone who is more deserving of your love and affection than you are yourself, and that person is not to be found anywhere. You, yourself, as much as anybody in the entire universe, deserve your love and affection."

Buddha

Love Thyself

Self-Love

Love thyself! Love for others can only be achieved if we embrace and can totally accept ourselves as we are. Unfortunately many of us hate our bodies, looks, emotions, memories, thoughts, even our lives. This is also greatly a fault of the education received within the family or society.

The current disappearance of family structure and consequently the visible lack of parental love have taken away the necessary nourishment for the growing child. In order to have a healthy sense of self, one must first receive love in an environment that fosters respect, compassion and nurturing. This is an absolute must if the person is to be a channel of love to others.

Healthy self-acceptance or self-love is not a form of narcissistic obsession with oneself, but the foundation of all love.

Patience and Self-Acceptance

When we realize that we live in a less-than-perfect universe in which everything—including how we view ourselves—changes, we grow in self-acceptance. Striving for perfection is good but it can be stressful for everyone around us including ourselves. There is a healthy as well as an unhealthy striving for perfection. As we grow stronger day by day, we need to have the patience of the bird that succeed in emptying an ocean, drop by drop, while she was looking for her lost eggs. Patience is essential for success.

In an unhealthy striving we feel urged forward out of fear of being average, or fear of not being good enough or not being liked. Impatience is thus a form of dislike or hate.

Approach your failings just as you would when dealing with a child that is falling while trying to learn how to walk.

Parental Influence

Lack of self-acceptance and self-love has manifold causes of which our parental influence is indeed only one, and yet one of the most powerful. Once violence or harshness has been ingested by a child, in any form, even if it was simply a withdrawal of love, it can later on take on a form of emotional vulnerability, instability, addictions, problems in their relationships, etc.

The child may not express violence in a physical way but may experience it and carry it internally. Someone may 'hear' the voices of those who were the greatest negative influences in her life echoing in their consciousness, pretending to be her own inner voice and telling her that she does not deserve something, or that she is not good enough, or that it is only when she is hurt that she will be loved. The roots of lack of self-love are deep.

Freedom From the Past

Loving and accepting oneself requires that we be kind in relation to our past mistakes and errors. Think of all the magnificent things ahead of you. There is no need to look back!

If we knew our vast potential, we would never spend even a moment brooding over our weaknesses or, at times, our troubled past, and we would work ever so more diligently and more enthusiastically towards our freedom.

Do not be a master-dweller on your past mistakes and do not hold yourself hostage to past misgivings, mistakes and temptations in which you might have failed. Bid good-bye to the past that has taught you so much about your real strengths and prepared you for your glorious future.

A Deeper Look Within Ourselves

Love is like any other skill that requires a proper education, training, intelligence and application. Just because we think that we are loving and that we have a great capacity for love, it does not automatically mean that we know how to love, how to express it, or even how to receive it.

Before we can understand and share love we must look deeply into ourselves. One of the particular issues in opening to love is that we become more vulnerable, and the hidden aspects of ourselves such as little fears and insecurities, jealousy, and impatience, may manifest to a greater degree, to our own surprise!

As we open our hearts the layers of our individuality with its strengths and weaknesses that lay buried deeply within get stirred up. The feelings of love then act like a cleansing agent and bring these aspects of our personality and emotions up to the surface.

These feelings and emotions are tied to our sense of security. This is where attachments form and become painful. They require a safe environment for their expression and processing.

Embrace them and accept them. If possible share your vulnerability with the person you love. Let trust gradually replace fear.

The Laws of Unity

Observe the phenomena in the world and you will see that every—even the tiniest—bit of suffering is due to lack of love. Even a single teardrop shed in anguish, an outcry of a homeless person forgotten and alone, a silent cry of Mother Nature who is hurting—all are due to humans having closed their hearts.

Any disharmony that may exist within us is also lived and experienced outside of us, the reason being that we are the Whole.

For example, your body may teach you a lesson in love. Has a limb, an organ, or a tiny cell in your body ever closed its 'heart' to the whole of your body?

Our evolution as human beings is the recognition of that Oneness and living according to its laws. Any straying away from the whole simply means inviting suffering to ourselves where we will be forced to embrace, to forgive and reunite. All our suffering is the result of the transgressions of the laws of love, which are the same as the laws of unity.

"*Love that is comforting coolness to those who burn with fire of suffering and passions; that is life-giving warmth to those abandoned in the cold desert of loneliness; to those who are shivering in the frost of a loveless world; to those whose hearts have become as if empty and dry by the repeated calls for help, by despair.*"

Buddha

Opening Your Heart

Mastering Love

In order to master love we need to broaden our definition of it and make it more extensive and spiritual in nature. We should first learn what exactly we are to love in another person or being. The spiritual nature of love teaches us and reminds us that it is our selves (as Pure Beings) that we love in other people. Just as we would like to receive love in a selfless and pure way, so we should try to extend it to others in the same way.

The practice of true love involves qualities such as giving, charity, compassion and forgiveness. These are all different forms of love. It is these qualities that we practice in the name of love.

The practice of compassion and forgiveness enables us to transcend our limited view of self and life, open our hearts, and break the shells of our little persons. Thus we are able to enter into another's heart, and live their life from inside of them, at least for a moment.

Healing Power of Love

In every heart there are stories of suffering and pain that nobody has ever heard. Carrying deep hidden wounds, their secrets unrevealed for the lack of a warm embrace of love that does not judge or reject, these beings often suffer in silence.

In every eye we meet, there is a world unspoken of, a world of unhealed memories of suffering, anguish, losses and pain, humiliation or abandonment, in need of understanding and a soft space that nurtures and heals. If in our love we can offer a buffer for their pain, and can master our listening, their suffering will be eased and their joy reclaimed.

Be the container, the soft space, and the nurturing mother of all beings in need of a refuge. Be ready to offer your heart as a gift, as a resting place for those in need. There is nothing like the heart that can contain all the anguish of a single sentient being. Such is the healing power of love!

Letting the Universe In

All offenses against love are offenses against Life, against evolution, and against enlightenment itself. We must learn to open our heart to embrace all, from the smallest and the 'insignificant' to the largest and 'most important', with no exception. It is a stupendous task . . . magnificent because even though we may doubt our capacity, we can never imagine how large our heart in fact is.

There, in the tiny space within the heart the whole universe rests, the life of which is sustained by the every pulse of our heart. If you want to be free you will have to take the whole universe with you, into your heart.

Compassionate Heart

"It is compassion that removes the heavy bar, opens the door to freedom, makes the narrow heart as wide as the world. Compassion takes away from the heart the inert weight, the paralyzing heaviness; it gives wings to those who cling to the lowlands of self. Compassion reconciles us to our own destiny by showing us the life of others, often much harder than ours." —Buddha

Just think for a moment of the suffering that some may be experiencing today—the endless streams of tears due to pain of a loss of a child, or a partner, or of silent suffering of someone who is without food, a friend, care or love.

How painful it must be to be forgotten by this world! Bring that person or being into your heart and offer them, with immense love and compassion, your heart as their refuge. Like a mother protecting her only child, ease their burden and wipe their tears.

Love and compassion, apart from enriching our own soul and heart, also enable us to forget our little bound up and limited self, characterized by self-obsession, excessive thinking about oneself and attachment. It is this little self that weighs us down, and blocks the free flow of energy and life.

Raising Our Awareness of Others

In order to reach the innermost chambers of somebody's heart, it is essential that our love be fresh like a running brook: never tiring, always giving. Yes, it may be that the people we know were with us yesterday, and the day before yesterday, but today, they are new people with new needs and new beauty.

Anything that is new fully engages our attention and it is the newness of that thing, something never previously perceived, that helps us discover new details about it.

One who is asleep to the presence of life in others, and who is not able to hear the powerful ticking of their souls, is asleep to the life in himself. In order to love one must raise his own awareness through selfless service of others and the practice of meditation.

Loving the Whole Creation

We first learn the 'baby form' of love—we love the closest members of our family, our partner, our friends, neighbors, the city we grew up in, the nation we were born in and, slowly, the whole world and ultimately the whole Creation. A sage is one who loves all and the reason being is that he or she feels no separation from others. A sage is one with all; a sage is in all.

Learning to Love All

"To live is to love. You live that you may learn to love."
—Sivananda

There is only one purpose in life—that is to learn to love all. All life challenges, diseases, addictions and suffering arise from one simple cause—from breaking this grand law of life, the law of Love. Every one of our problems can be traced to a lack of love, the love that is being held tightly within the heart.

To love all is indeed the most daunting demand of the Spirit within. The sooner we come to accept what we are asked to do, the quicker will be our realization that we are All.

Love Thy Neighbor

Spirituality is nothing but broadening our understanding of our connectedness with all. In practice it means expanding and mastering our love. The difference between an ordinary person and a sage is that the ordinary person lives in his own prison of limited and separate self whereas the sage lives in All.

Jesus was the embodiment of the Supreme Love, and so were Buddha and every other great sage that has ever walked on this earth. All their teachings could be put together in one phrase:

Love Thy Neighbor as Thyself

At the end of life the most important question will be: How deep and strong was your love?

Love and Identification

The level of identification with any being is the measure of our love. Identification means that something outside of us has now become us. To identify is to become. We have transferred the sense of our self onto something outside of us. In identification we extend the sense of who we are. The person or the object we identify with becomes a part of our own identity and naturally we would do the same good things for that person as we would do for ourselves. The greater the identification, the greater the love.

On the path of love we learn to identify with others and gradually increase this identification to a larger number of beings through selfless service along with the contemplation of Oneness so that we can eventually include all beings in our embrace. Whatever we see, touch, and hear is us in that particular form.

Purity of Heart

"Love is the divine force of this universe. The purer you make your heart, the greater will be the power of your love. Be kind, be compassionate, be humble, be tolerant, be good, be just, be natural. Love the eternal in every being. Make no distinctions between one being and another."
—Sivananda

Purity of heart is the condition for perfection in love. A pure heart is the fountain of all goodness and the very source of Infinite Love. To purify means to refine, to remove any coarseness from all, including the smallest of our actions. Purification means eradication of the personal ego-element and the removal of all negative emotions and instinctive urges from our nature, from our actions, and seeing the Divine in all.

Love is recognition of the One Reality that dwells in all hearts. Let your speech, look, touch, sentiment and thought become gradually refined so as to reflect the Oneness. Speak, act and think as if others were your own self.

Oneness

"One should analyze oneself. You should have a large heart. Become one with the entire mankind. You should share with others what you have. Every day, as soon as you get up, ask yourself: "How many good actions was I able to do yesterday?" and resolve to excel the previous day in doing good to others. Thus would you evolve rapidly?"
—Sivananda

A spiritual aspirant should feel even more deeply for others, and want to serve them and help them be freed from their suffering. Spiritual masters serve all humanity, all beings and the whole Creation, and urge their students to do the same. Being established in the perception of Oneness they teach by example.

Without service and giving of oneself there is no love. Love must vibrate in action.

Whatever the yoga, whatever the name, whatever the stages of Self-realization and progress there may be—there exists only one end and that is the realization of Oneness. Oneness, selflessness and unconditional love, incessant kindness and infinite gratitude are all synonyms. There are infinite ways to express, realize, live and become that one Unifying Principle, the one 'Substance' of this Creation that holds all beings together, the Self that is made of Bliss. Let us call it love. Let us learn fast what true love is. One cannot go wrong by learning how to love.

How Pure Is Your Love?

Your life is measured by your love for different things—objects, people, particular types of skills, art forms, or anything. The greater the love, the greater the identification with a particular thing we love.

Love enables the breaking of the illusory boundary that exists seemingly between 'other' and us. As the result of this process, we gain the knowledge of that which we love—since we are able to enter into it. This explains why the saints and sages who have cosmic consciousness know everything. They are able to 'enter' everything and it is their love that enabled them to do so.

The key to this experience is selflessness—an incessant giving of oneself for the sake of others.

Selfless Service

The essence of love is giving and sacrifice. Selflessness in its fullness is the same as Ishwara Consciousness. We see it present in all saints and sages. They see Oneness in all and treat even the smallest unit of consciousness, or the smallest being as sacred.

The operation of the law of Karma, which is the reaction set up by Creation in response to our deviation from Dharma or selflessness, is nothing but a curative for selfishness or ego, and a means for bringing us back to the Absolute Reality or God. In order to grow spiritually we have no choice but to expand and we can only succeed in it if we open our hearts. This is also the reason why the spiritual traditions first teach selfless activity.

Love in Action

"Live a life of utter devotion to service. Fill your heart with fervor and enthusiasm for service. Live only to be a blessing to others. If you want to achieve this you will have to refine your mind. You will have to polish your character. You will have to mould or build your character. You should develop sympathy, affection, benevolence, tolerance and humility."
—Sivananda

Life is fully lived only when we strive to bring goodness and joy into the others' lives, by sharing what we have and know with our sisters and brothers - with the whole humanity. The urge that springs from the heart to remove someone's sadness and lighten their difficult day, offer a hope and consolation and bring a smile to a face worn out by the vicissitudes of life is a precious gift and a blessing.

Give Your Love

To grow in love is to grow in selflessness and purity. We all have the capacity for Infinite Love since in our hearts there is already a memory, an awareness of—however remotely it may be felt at times—Infinite Reality. Infinite Reality is nothing but the Infinite Existence, Knowledge and Love.

Start by being kind to yourself and remember that you can only grow one tiny step at a time. Life is full of small steps, infinite beginnings and magical possibilities. Our life is the chance we give to every present moment. No saintly soul lives either in the past or in the future, ever. Our life is contained in a moment. We live in a moment; our Love must also be that of the moment.

Do not wait until tomorrow for circumstances to get better or to give of yourself, as you may become fatigued by the day's challenges and pressures. Choose today, and among so many moments of today, choose this very moment to give of your love. The Now is the cradle of new beginnings, discoveries and of new, loving and kind actions for others. Our progress lies in utilizing every moment for flight to a new dimension. What a joy it is to live for others!

Helping Others

Let us meditate today on one common Reality.
What is the source of love, kindness, empathy, sympathy
or even altruism?

What is the connective thread between all beings that is
behind all so-called positive action, service or help?
We see the fire brigades, the police and the ambulances
all rush to alleviate suffering and save lives. When we see
somebody in need of help, such as a person who has just
had an accident, or when somebody falls on the ground—
we immediately feel moved to help. We act like a mother
whose child has been suddenly hurt.

Do we know where this urge comes from? Have we ever
contemplated what makes us want to help somebody?

This drive arises from the deepest place in our heart.
There is a sudden 'recognition' that there is one life, one
consciousness. The urge to assuage the suffering of another
is immediate; it does not question. It happens so rapidly
that it transcends the thinking process. This force proceeds
from our heart, not from the conscious mind. The heart
is the center of Oneness. We are ready to sacrifice for
'another'. There is no 'I'. Action becomes inaction. There is
a Union on the level of Being. Helping others is a powerful
'reaction' to the existence of the common Reality in both—
us and the person or persons concerned.

Kundalini and Service

A person who has even a partial awakening of the Kundalini Shakti will feel an urge to serve the whole Creation since the Kundalini Shakti is the energy of the (whole) Creation. A person with a completely awakened kundalini does not see himself or herself separate from others any longer.

Kundalini awakening is the same as Samadhi (superconscious state). Kundalini is not a 'personal' energy; it does not belong to you or me. It is cosmic energy and at the time of awakening there is a consummation of the whole process of yoga, and the so-called 'personality' or the separate sense of 'I' as we know it, dissolves completely. The 'body' of such an awakened person becomes the place (temple) in which all the energy of the universe converges, and thus the cosmically awakened consciousness of the 'person' becomes one with the will of God and his or her actions are no longer 'normal' human actions but the manifestation of the law of Dharma.

The Dharma of Kindness

Deliberate acts of kindness practiced at all times is key to developing infinite or cosmic love. Love cannot exist without kindness. The whole world rests on kindness, which is just one form of Dharma.

When true kindness is enkindled in our heart it then 'crosses the borders' of our limited personality or a small circle of friends and family. It gradually starts to include more until it is able to include all.

Kindness is like a soft mantle of gentleness, tactfulness and consideration. In moments of kindness we offer our own heart as a meeting place of goodness and benevolence, or as a cooling refuge from the heat of another beings' suffering and the scorching intensity of their life. With our mind free from judgment and ready to embrace them completely, we rest in that mantle of connectedness.

In kindness we cherish every moment with that person or the being concerned as if it were our last, and as if that person were the most beloved of all. Meditate on kindness, practice kindness—become the embodiment of kindness.

Kindheartedness

Kindness is the secret of love, and spiritual life is nothing but the perfection of love expressed in the smallest of details of our actions. The perfection of this love is found in the practice of unlimited kindness.

Kindness means making someone feel loved, understood and accepted. In addition kindness enriches our knowledge about our own mind and it ennobles our Soul.

We exercise kindheartedness when we descend with deep sympathy into the hearts of others, ordinary people, children, the old and the sick, the homeless, and the suffering, and can actually feel the depth of their anguish.

We speak with softness and express tenderly our feelings, thoughts and attitudes with care and understanding.

We can make kindness a substratum of our cooking, cleaning, and handling things and machines. This requires mastery and control of our own thoughts and emotions.

We also look at the sunrise, nature, the sky and the trees, rocks and grass and feel the earth and the breeze and all other elements with kindness, joy and gratitude. Isn't that love too?

Kindness Blossoms in Your Heart

Where kindness is present, there is absence of desire to domineer over others and monopolize their time, presence and energy and use them for the sake of our own pleasure or for enhancing the sense of our own greatness or power. When your heart longs to see others happy just as you would want to see your own happiness, then know that kindness has blossomed in your heart

"*Love possesses not nor would it be possessed;*
For love is sufficient unto love...
And think not you can direct the course of love, for love, if it
finds you worthy, directs your course.
Love has no other desire but to fulfill itself."

Kahlil Gibran

Love Or Attachment

The Need for Love

We all have the same need—to love and be loved. And we all struggle to find the real meaning of love throughout our lives. Our understanding and the meaning of love changes as we move through different stages of our lives and grow and expand spiritually.

The experience of suffering and the practice of gratitude season our love. We struggle to understand what love is because although it is completely natural to feel, express and receive love, we get confused since a lot of what we call love is mixed with attachment. In most any form of love, we have this strange mix.

What would our lives look like if we could express and manifest total love and if all our thoughts, words and deeds emerged from the bottomless ocean of mercy and compassion?

The Nature of Attachment

The distinction must be made between sensual love and a higher form of love, and between attachment and selfless love.

Attachment is created through a process of intense thinking about an object or a person whereby our mind gets magnetized by the quality/qualities of the person or the object. Among many possible qualities that a person or an object can have, the mind gives a special value to only those qualities that it sees and admires in the object. Then it starts to exaggerate them. The person or the object is thus seen through the prism of exaggeration in as much the same way as when we look at something through a microscope. In this way we create an imbalanced view of an object or a person. The more we think about the object the more desirable the object becomes.

Self-Centered Love

In the ordinary form of love, which hardly can be called as such (since it is often mixed with attachment and selfishness), a person's usual focus is, perhaps unconsciously, the achievement of one's own happiness and pleasure.

Even though we may be earnest and working hard to make somebody happy, we are truly doing it for the sake of our own self. Wanting to make another person happy often masquerades our own desire to see that person as our own source of pleasure and happiness, and therefore we want something back from that person. Such 'love' does not have the other person's happiness as a goal in reality, but it is self-centered. The mechanism behind this is rather subtle.

Self-centered love is perpetually strained by effort. The attachment is nothing but seeking pleasure through a medium of an object or a person.

Attachment is about me, and love is about you.

Love and the Ego

Love is the cosmic process of discovering our self as the Self of All. Our separation from others is only apparent or illusory, unreal at the core, because our consciousness is severely limited by us strongly identifying with the physical body. Therefore, in loving others we really love our own Self.

The Self here in question is not physical, emotional or mental—it is rather the true Self, which is the deepest level of our Being manifested as Pure Awareness or Consciousness. Love and the Being are identical.

Because we don't know the true nature of our connection with others, our ordinary experience of love often seems limited. The love that is born in our hearts belongs to All, therefore only giving of oneself to others through selfless service of and loving All justifies the true definition of love. Naturally that is easier said than done. The ego adamantly stands in the way.

Difference Between Attachment and Love I

Attachment is infatuation with somebody's qualities and/ or with his or her name and form. It is a superimposition of the idea, "This person/object (and their qualities), will be the cause of my happiness." The 'objective' is the pleasure we expect to receive from the person to whom we are attached. It is not about loving the other person.

As our minds (as well as the external world) are ever-changing, no single person can be a perpetual source of pleasure for anybody. We will discover that attachment is not love but it is about self-pleasure. Yet for most of us the first form of love is a mix of attachment and love.

Difference Between Attachment and Love II

Attachment is an inverted form of love (for oneself) masking itself as love for another. Attachment has certain conditions or agendas set in relationship to the person or object of love. Once the condition is not fulfilled, the love diminishes, and the person may look for another object of love.

The greater the attachment, the more acute and intense are the demands asked, usually unconsciously, of the object of love. Thus through the medium of the very conditions set by the attached persons themselves, they soon find themselves in the state of dependence.

Love is for love's sake. It never asks for anything, it does not reason, it is its own gift; it has its own glory and beauty. It beautifies the one who loves as well as the beloved. Attachment is limited; love has no limits. Whereas attachment is effortful and full of anxious striving to please in order to receive, love flows effortlessly. Attachment is for a particular; love is for all.

Difference Between Attachment and Love III

When the person you love becomes the very periphery or the limit of your affection, know that to be an attachment. Your love has become limited like the space in a box. Love by its very nature is expansive and cannot be contained, and it is meant to be given freely to all, yet it has now become confined to only one person.

The nature of love is that it is boundless and boundary-less. It is like a space with no limit. True love is inclusive of all. Make the love you feel for one person a center of your affection and let the whole universe be the boundary. Let the whole universe into your heart. This is a spiritual definition of love.

Break Free From the Pattern of Attachment I

A tool that spiritual aspirants use to free themselves from attachment is discriminative power called Viveka. Attachment is a belief that things don't change, or if they do one simply cannot accept that as fact. Non-attachment does not mean not having. We are simply not dependent on something else for our happiness. And it helps first of all, to know who we are!

Viveka is the cognitive process of discrimination. It is the sword that cuts through the mesh of attachments. It is derived from the root 'vic', which means 'to separate'. Through the power of discrimination we see, moment by moment, that everything (including our body and mind) is subject to change and so what we see are not solid objects but processes as such, and that which does not change, the presence within us in the form of Awareness or Consciousness, enables us to know ourselves as distinct from what we observe.

That changeless Awareness has been there before you were even born.

The understanding and the recognition that this Awareness is ever present is what helps us establish a non-attached attitude towards everything.

Break Free From the Pattern of Attachment II

We can't break free until we are able to see, through the eye of discrimination, the pain that is caused by attachment, and that the joy that it takes out of love is actually often mixed with attachment. Due to the pressure of Karma, one is attracted to a particular object, person or whatever it may be. Karma is the pull, a force of everything behind every action in nature, including our own life. Attachment is the hardest thing to break ever.

Discrimination is the king of all cognitive processes and applying the discriminative process is in itself the key to resolving the problem of our earthly existence. The first step is to bring in a laser light-like discrimination and inquiry by asking:

"What are the consequences of attachments?"

Attachment has two, often invisible concomitants—anger and fear of loss. Whatever we become attached to, we will be afraid to lose and whatever stands in the way of our enjoyment will be the cause of anger. Therefore, we can say that the subtle causes of our fear and anger are attachments.

Break Free From the Pattern of Attachment III

The next step in cultivating discrimination is to cultivate a certain healthy distance from objects, people and situations.

"Love less, but love long," says Swami Sivananda. Once you lessen your grip on objects, people and circumstances, and have lessened the desire to control them, you will start to experience a new form of freedom, the inner freedom that is infinitely vaster than the so-called freedom of ordinary people. It is such freedom that can equally nourish others with what they need in order to grow and evolve. In this type of freedom you will be able let go of dwelling on the either too desirable or the undesirable traits in others, the traits that may cause you to either get attached to or dislike someone. You will develop equanimity. You will start to recognize and appreciate the true beauty and unique nature of everybody.

Break Free From the Pattern of Attachment IV

Let us give some praise to discrimination itself. Spiritual discrimination is the eye of wisdom, the mystical eye of knowledge of Lord Siva, the sword of Goddess Durga. It is a rare gift earned through the eons of selfless giving for the benefit and wellbeing of others.

Another contemplation is this one:
"What is the nature of this world, including us as body/ mind complexes?" The answer is CHANGE. We live in an ever-changing world and yet we are looking for stability and constancy. We are trying to find the non-existent tooth of a crow. Even though intellectually we may know and admit that everything is in constant flux, emotionally we have no strength to accept this and thus we would like to immortalize the forms and names, us and others in the physical form. We try our best to make this world of transitory values a permanent abode of our sentiments and happiness. We have never deeply contemplated this word—change.

"Love sees with faultless vision, judges with true judgment,
acts in wisdom. Look through the eyes of Love, and you shall
see everywhere the Beautiful and the True; judge with the
mind of Love, and you shall err not, shall wake no wail of
sorrow; act in the spirit of Love, and you shall strike eternal
harmonies upon the Harp of Life."

James Allen

Meditations On Love

Gestures of Love

Love is mastered only through the practice and the expression of love.

One of the greatest practices of love is that of acceptance. There are different levels of mastery of this practice. Acceptance can only arise when our mind is free from the tendency to objectify, to project ideas, and to control.

It is only in a calm and reflective mind that true love is born. In that state we have an intuitive feeling that behind all the apparent differences we are commonly aware of, there is a common principle that unites us—that of one life, one Light, and one Consciousness.

A good way to practice acceptance is to use the power of smile. How beautifully can this principle of Oneness unfold when we are able to forget our body, and connect with another person through a smile? The recognition of the presence of another person is best manifested through smiling. There is a miracle in a smile. You can use it with confidence. A smile has the power to confer trust. It beatifies, adds softness, heals and can be a container for others' suffering. In simple words it is a gesture of love!

Love Begins With Oneself

Our relationships with others begin with, and are the reflection of how we relate to ourselves.

Begin your practice of self-acceptance from early in the day. Sit in a favorite meditative posture. Start concentrating on your breath or a mantra such as Om or any holy word. Observe your mind with the intention of accepting the thoughts and feelings as they arise, ever so gently and patiently. Then let each one go, swiftly, without holding onto any. Each time you let go of thought bring your mind back to your breath or a mantra. Again and again, without looking for an end to the rumbling of the mind, simply embrace it, and then let go.

First observe and listen deeply to the various layers of your being, thoughts, feelings and sensations, gradually comprehending their nature. Then comes acceptance, embracing with no judgment and letting go.

This practice should gradually be extended further into the day until your practice becomes habitual and natural and it can literally last all day long. This may take several years, but you need not worry about it.

The next step is to apply the same to others. We try to enter into the various dimensions of another being, trying to fathom their experience from within their own inner world.

Listen deeply. The same steps follow—listening, accepting, embracing and letting go.

Every victory in developing compassion and acceptance for our own mistakes and negative states of mind will reflect and increase our ability to accept other peoples' negative mental states.

Starting Your Day With Love

Our first practice in the morning should be that of tuning to the deepest essence of who we are as human beings. That essence is of the nature of Deep Silence of Presence within our heart. This practice can take a form of meditation or prayer followed by the further reflection on how we can deepen our connection with all beings in this vast universe. Then we may want to take a vow that we will unite with all beings in our hearts, and be ready to help with our hands and think the best thoughts for others in our minds. As we embrace this day we vow to not leave anybody out of our love's reach.

We may not have much success on the first day or as the days go by, but as a first step, we must learn to strengthen our thought forms and intentions, and protect them from negative thinking and deterioration.

We vow to practice kindness and work hard to promote a greater harmony with others and the many beings of the universe this very day.

Meditations on Love

- Love for our dearest ones.
  (They come first since they are the easiest to love.)

- Love for those who perhaps have given you more than you were able to appreciate, such as your teachers or neighbors.

- Love for those whose suffering is obvious: the afflicted, poor, sick, dying, or abandoned beings.

- Love for the people towards whom we have neutral or no feelings.

- Love for those who may dislike us or even hate us— those we may hurt in some ways.

- Love for those who may have hurt us and thus we may have coincidentally made into our enemies.

- Love for Nature: Love for animals, fish, rocks, plants, flowers, bushes.

- Love for mountains, hills, oceans, rivers, lakes, the sky.

- Love for the Earth, Sun and the Moon, all the planets and the whole universe.

- Love for the Creator of this wonderful world and the Creator of our lives.

Meditation on the Sacred Heart

Visualize your heart as the heart of Jesus, or Buddha or Swami Sivananda or any other saint you admire. Their hearts are full of clear Light. Feel that your heart is filled with the same clear Light. This Light is the essence of all compassion, goodness and Bliss.

Visualize different kinds of beings—those in need of refuge, warmth, compassion, or simply an embrace (you may start with concrete images of people you know, animals, etc.)— being drawn to your heart's vast expanse of Light.

Your heart is opening wide to welcome them all. Let everyone now find their place in the vast embrace of your warmth, kindness and softness. Let them settle in. Then let them pour out all their sadness, powerlessness, ignorance and despair, their losses and disappointments, into your heart's vast expanse. Now let their suffering melt and be transformed into the pure Light of wisdom and kindness. You can feel their relief and the healing that has taken place.

At the end visualize that all these beings are truly nothing but yourself in many different forms. They may have entered your heart as 'outsiders' in the first stage of the practice but now the boundary that separates you from them has melted away and there is only one Being, the Being of joy. It is all one. Feel yourself as one with all.

Loving All Qualities in Others

Love is a great purifier. It opens all visible and invisible areas within our mind and the whole body and the mind receives, like a gentle shock, an awakening.

The first step in love involves recognizing the unique nature of another person as if it were the Creator's intention that has been revealed to us. Each person comes into this life with a peculiar mix of strengths and weaknesses, beautiful aspects and vulnerabilities. Then comes the acceptance of the totality of that person.

Naturally the challenge is to be able to love the whole person and not only the beautiful or amusing aspects of her or him.

Acknowledge Others in a New Way

It is in others' 'presence' that we discover our own presence. Love is the 'meeting' of one Being in two different bodies and reflected through the medium of two minds. It is the same Light of consciousness that shines equally in both beings.

Next comes listening.

Listen with your whole heart to the content of their words and look for the non-verbal expressions of their being, whether that is a person, a child, an animal or even a tree, or a rock. They all have their own unique language.

Let the communion now take place between you and them, leaving yourself, your opinions, your interpretations out. It is in the absence of our self-importance and in giving a full focus to their inner experience that their confidence and trust in us, which are nothing but forms of love, are born.

Listening With Your Heart

Recognize the presence of every being you meet. Make them feel special and listened to. There may be in their heart a secret they could not share out of fear of being misunderstood. Help them share their innermost longings.

Have you ever listened with your heart?
Have you ever listened to another person's heart?

What a joy!

You will hear . . . the stream of time . . .the mixed sounds of joy and suffering etched in the depths of memories buried within the vast space of her soul. Now the Soul speaks to the Soul.

What is love but the pulsating of hearts in unison—all merging in the Silence?

Becoming One With Others

You may start the practice of giving love to others by superimposing the idea that you live in and through another person, that you exist in their body and mind, feel their thoughts, move their hands and feet, and feel that their heart is your heart. You can try to visualize what it may feel like to exist in another being. Great empathy and a heart full of kindness will arise as you feel their struggles as your own, and their joys as your own joys.

As you are practicing feeling Oneness with others and identifying with them, you will notice that with a child you feel just like that child, with an old person you feel the weight of his or her old age in their body, pain or joy, or wisdom, and you are able to fathom the depth of their life experience, and with the sick and dying, you feel their illness as if you were dying. When you are with any person you are like just that person. There you are—on the path to cosmic consciousness!

Expressing Our Love

There are infinite ways to express love!

Creativity in our expression of love is the key to its life, nourishment and constancy. If our inner world is stagnant, we will not be able to step out of the way we in which we ordinarily perceive others and their lives, and we will not be able to love them fully. We will be seeing them 'in the past' as somebody we know 'all too well' that now we don't 'see' them any longer.

The secret of spirituality is knowing how to always be fresh and new. This precious drop of freshness in the way we look at somebody, talk to him or her, feel them and relate to them as though it is the very first time we have ever seen them, is the key to loving them ever afresh, and to feeling the thrill of sharing the gift of life with others.

Love is a Spiritual Discipline

True love is not about having a good time and enjoying what others and we can give to each other. Just like with other forms of yoga, love in its higher form involves the eradication of the sense of ego. Pure love can be awakened in many ways.

Steps to awaken pure love:

1) We are fortunate enough to meet a great master who is the embodiment of unconditional love and who can lead us to the experience of transcending the little self (ego).

2) We raise our understanding of love to that of all-inclusiveness. The process of the expansion of the heart takes place gradually. We become aware that no being should be left remain outside of our love's reach. For example, one may love his or her pet but may not feel the same love for a homeless person. We are ready to sacrifice our time or money for our pets, but we do not feel the urge and necessity to provide a meal for another human being.

3) Combine love with service; love that is limited in its expression, either quantitatively or qualitatively, cannot blossom. Service enlivens and vivifies love. Love is like a seed and service is that which nurtures the seed. Love without service is barren of essence.

4) We maintain a sacred attitude in our service to others.

Love as Yoga

Love is a form of yoga; love is meditation; love is identification; love is realization. It may appear that the objective of love is another being but if we look at love as an experience more deeply, we will come to the conclusion that the object of our love is, in fact, our own Self.

A Reflection

Hold back, oh mind, when you see the faults in others! Why be so surprised at peoples' failings as if this world were an abode of heavenly bliss and perfection? Why should you, oh mind, be surprised at the fallibility of human nature? You yourself, oh mind, may have been reveling, not long ago, in the same dust and mud of error, and stumbled numerous times, wondering if there was a way out.

Why do other peoples' struggles seem so trivial to you, oh mind, their struggles that have now become your victories. Desist and forbear my friend, from seeing evil in others!

The one who is failing now will be a saint tomorrow— that is the law of the Eternal Being. Nobody has been permanently sentenced to remain in this dark prison of persistent flaws. Everybody has a bright future. Yours is to see that Light in others!

Make a Vow

Don't give up watching your mind during the day simply because it has 'betrayed' you in some way, or has become agitated, fearful or negative. It is in these moments that your compassion is crucial. Generally it does not take a long time before an untrained mind gives up the practice and it becomes frustrated because it has 'failed' again in succumbing to negative thoughts.

Take heart and let yourself rest in the holy process of self-observation and self-acceptance each time you find that the mind has 'strayed' from being steady, loving or peaceful.

"The first test of love is that it knows no bargaining. So long as you see a person love another only to get something from her, you know that that is not love. Love is always the giver and never the taker. The second test is that love knows no fear. Where do you ever see love in fear? With love never comes the idea of fear."

Swami Vivekananda

Evolving Towards True Love

The True Test of Love

Love does not mean the perception of only goodness, beauty, power, elegance, charm and other charismatic features in somebody. In fact we could say that love with its own preferences is a 'biased' kind of love that may dwindle away if any of the qualities were to be reduced or lost.

True love recognizes and accepts the whole person, not only the good qualities but also even the weaknesses of others. And therein lies the test of our love. When a person with weaknesses is 'allowed' to first of all own them, to work through them and make even small steps to eradicate or sublimate them, then the person needs to see that we have created a buffer, a container to support them in their struggle. We are there for them if they fall and more importantly we should be there to honor and praise the efforts—however small—they may be making. We know that changing bad habits takes will, time and the patience of others.

Love Free From Fear

As long as you see somebody as different and separate from you, even if it were your child, you cannot truly love him or her in the true sense of the word: true Love that is free from attachment or fear. All love is by definition a Union, or better to say, the experience of Oneness.

True Love

It is very humbling that despite all the years of our experience in loving others we discover that we still don't know what love is. And it should be like that so that we continue to learn about ourselves from others. Those who believe that they truly love and yet the world seems to be opposing them are living in confusion.

As your love gets more perfected, so the world starts to shine in new colors and respond to your love. Even nature will obey a person who truly loves.

Forms of Love

Love is a complex experience initially comprised of many different types of sentiments, mixed levels of understanding, degrees of identification and of Bliss. Eventually the experience of love culminates in the experience of deep silence of (one) inner Self. The experience of love varies among individuals as per their stage of evolution.

We can explain this by using the model of three bodies (physical, astral and causal) or five sheaths (food, prana, mind, intellect and Bliss) in yoga. The five sheaths rest within the three bodies. Love is variously experienced in different inner sheaths as its mediums, from the physical to the causal. The sheaths also represent different degrees of subtlety of matter. The expression of love is reflected differently in each sheath. As we mature spiritually, we move from the purely physical sensation of love to a subtler, more refined form of love and eventually to the most sublime experience of love. This highest form of empirical love is on the level of the blissful sheath (the causal body). At the very end, even this sheath is transcended and the subject and the object (of love) merge. This is nothing but the Pure Consciousness, or the state of Self-realization. And this form can only be reached through a purified form of love called devotion or Bhakti.

Love and the Ego

The problems of both achieving the Supreme state of meditation as well as that of true love are related to the existence of this mysterious agent called ego, or the sense of one's isolated self. The birth of either the sublime state of meditation, or of love, means the death of ego.

The ego creates a peculiar sense of distance in relation to its object, or a person, even when that person is the one it 'loves'. The role of ego is to assert, to separate, to distance, to hold a particular notion, or have an opinion about something or somebody. It thinks that everything should either 'belong to me' or in some way 'be related to me'. The life and the robustness of ego depend on how well it can keep itself distanced and isolated through its notions, superimpositions and opinions, on which it thrives well.

In our practice of listening to another person, we are endeavoring to put aside this assertive tendency of our ego. We are learning to be simply opinion-less for the time being. We allow for the truth of the other person's words or the state of their heart or mind to manifest freely without us infringing on, altering or manipulating it in any way. In this way we can learn to discriminate between the truth and an opinion.

Love and Understanding

Humility and respect are important qualities to be developed by aspiring loving spiritual beings. We should accept that we might not always know the best way to express our love for someone even though that person may be very close to us. Sometimes the best approach is to first cultivate simple respect for him or her, knowing that every person has the right of existence on their own as per Creator's 'wish'. We must also try to develop an understanding of the person, and not worry about loving as such, for the time being.

Without understanding a person we cannot love him or her. The love will come in due time.

Give Your Love Freely

Love that is unspoken or unshared, love that is bereft of sentiment and meaning, love that lacks warmth and joyful expression—is not love. Love that others cannot read or understand and that is not properly communicated, love that is not spirited and does not stir the other person to goodness—we may reevaluate it to see whether it is truly love.

Banish all fear that your love may not be reciprocated or even understood. So what if it isn't? Asking for love to be returned is not love but a form of a bargain, conditioning, a protection that the little self is trying to secure for itself.

Let your love be free. Let others bathe in your love. To love is to continually give.

When you love, you are giving an expression to your Ultimate Nature. Love can never fail in its effect regardless of how long it may take to transform the being or the matter it touches.

There is no other magic in life but love. It is only when we look at the world through the eyes of love that we see magic everywhere. The greater the selflessness, the greater the love and the degree of Bliss that we experience. What we are hoping to achieve in every act of love is to forget ourselves!

Love and Freedom

In the heart of every being these two merge: love and freedom. Love and freedom are synonyms. To love, one has to be free.

When we are internally bound by our own emotions, our opinions and little 'truths' we cannot help but want to control the other person. Instead of giving love we keep on projecting our own little world of insecurities onto others and expect that the others will simply 'fill the hole'.

Through yoga, self-analysis and meditation you can learn to gradually free yourself from the tyranny of all negative aspects of the mind (fear, anger, hatred, lust, jealousy and other emotions) that impinge themselves on your own and other people's freedom. An unfree person lives in the prison of his own mind and does his best to 'keep' others enslaved along with him. Freedom is the freedom from all limitations including all thoughts and everything that lies outside of our Awareness or Consciousness.

Religion of the Heart

"The only true religion is the religion of love or the religion of heart. Feel for others as you feel for yourself. Love expects no reward. Love knows no fear. Love Divine gives—does not demand. Love thinks no evil; imputes no motive. To love is to share and serve." —Sivananda

Just like a mother who, because of her deep love, does not expect anything from her children, so also true Love does not expect any remuneration from the so-called object of love.

Love is its own reward. Love knows no fear as it does not see anything outside of it. You have no fear of your arm because it is one with you. Similarly great masters love everybody deeply because they feel one with all and thus live fearless lives.

Search for Love, Live Love

Love means life. Let us awaken to the great life pulsing in all forms, in the whole Creation. Let the touch of our love awaken the life, the Awareness, the Bliss in all those we meet, especially in those whose hopes may have been hushed by their suffering or a loss of direction.

Let our Being kindle love in every form our eyes see, in every sound our ears hear, every figure that our hands touch, every realm that our thoughts can reach, and every sister-soul that our Soul knows as itself. To love one must awaken to the totality of life and not only in isolated moments in time. Love asks for the complete awakening to life. Just as you feel life pulsating in every cell of your body, so also one who has mastered Love feels life pulsating in every inch of Creation. He feels that the whole Creation is his body. Search for love, find love, express love and live love.

How to See Others

When we look at a person what do we see?
Do we see the person from within her?
Can we try to see the person with eyes of the whole Creation?

We often see nothing but the projections of our own mind, our biases, fears, expectations and at times something to admire in her. Our seeing is not really seeing; it is the repetition of what we know, of what we have learned by experience, by habit—it is the seeing of others through the prism of our own conditioning.

It is certainly hard to see others in a new way, every day, nay every moment, because it is difficult to think in a fresh way. It requires practice and a spiritual outlook. We must learn to let a person 'speak' his or her own being and heart, be his or her unique self, and not try to speak our own thoughts and prejudices through that person. Love is learning to see others through the eyes of Cosmic Mother. Then we will see so much more in everybody than we see now.

Freedom from Judgements

The secret of love is freedom from judgment. A judging mind cannot love since the object of its love is made to conform to the demands of such a mind. The person we love is not given freedom to be. To judge is to superimpose ideas, opinions, values and qualities that are not intrinsic to the nature of that which is observed. Judging others is to interpret what we see from a selfish perspective. It is trying to put a limit on their nature or trying to modify it.

Judgment is often followed by a desire to control the other person. Not judging does not mean that another can do anything they like. There is always space for a healthy exchange and communication between people. It needs to be created. It does not come overnight. It is the result of hard work on oneself and the relationship. Instead of judgment offer a loving word that comes from your heart or a thought that is in the interest of another's growth.

All beings should be given the freedom to express their basic nature as long as their freedom does not transgress the laws of Oneness or unity, and does not infringe upon the basic freedom of others.

Self-Obsession

Another secret of love is to not use the word 'I' much when you are with another person. Just try to notice how frequently you refer to the 'I' in your daily language and thoughts. You will simply be amazed by the fact that most of our thinking has this 'I' as its target.

We are concerned with whether the little 'I' is comfortable enough or not, we plan what we are going to do next to make the little 'I' happy. The little 'I' notices others only after it has made itself comfortable. This self-obsession, which may also be very subtle, has closed the doors of entry to others.

Where 'I' or 'me' exists, others do not. This little 'I' gives rise to numerous superficial thoughts in the mind, giving no rest to the thinker.

You may want to try taking a vow of not talking about yourself unless needed, at least for a day, and you will discover that the whole of your mind and the Soul have become refreshed and quiet. Let others be the focus of your thoughts and service for the time being.

The Pitfalls of Self-Cherishing

In order to learn to love, we need to take ourselves out of the process of listening to and trying to understand others.

Love is the process of learning about others but it is also learning about ourselves through others.

It is in self-forgetfulness that the seed of love is born and also nurtured. In giving to others we too are the receivers of the greatest gift—that of love. It is as if the receiver immediately reflects the love back to the one who gives it. It is a sense of self-importance that is the real thief in any relationship—it steals away the love and its joy.

We tend to believe, perhaps unconsciously, that everything should have some connection with and relevance to us—in short we believe that we are the most important. One needs just a little more honesty to notice this. In this process of self-cherishing we tend to relate every experience, and especially the experiences of others to ourselves.

We ask silently, "What is in it for me?" We are the hubs around which everything turns. Then naturally listening to others and loving others becomes the problem. The listening is then more about us than having a rapport with others.

Gestures of Love

Love begins with a smile. A smile is a form of warmth, an emanation of inner glow and spirit. Nature is full of beautiful smiles—even among flowers and animals we see smiles. Amidst humans, some of the most beautiful smiles are those of babies, women, mothers, old people, and of course, the sages.

For as long as the muscles on our faces are tight and strained, we remain inwardly contracted and are not able to open our hearts to other beings. A smile is an indirect language of your heart. It has a healing effect especially on those who are stricken by suffering of some kind.

Let us master the informal ways of love in the form of gestures. Let our heart speak first through kind looks, smiles and gentleness, courtesy and understanding. In this way we would have greatly helped the world too.

In Closing

There is a place deep within your heart that knows no sorrow, no doubt, no exhaustion, no desire, no fulfillment, no restlessness. It is the region of silent presence that knows no abandonment or hurt.

In that ocean of peace, bliss and love there is nothing left to be understood, nobody to forgive, nothing to feel ashamed of.

It is the place that has burnt all shame, fear, anger and lust to ashes. It is forever free from thoughts, mental constructs and imaginations of any kind.

That is who you truly are, my brothers and sisters, that is who I am and who all beings are in their essence. This is also the innermost nature of our once-upon-a-time enemy. It is the One space that now embraces all. Everything has now entered into me, the me that knows no boundary.

Salutations to that Being! Salutations to that Being in all!

Glossary

Note: The eternal aspect of all beings and the whole creation is called Pure Consciousness; it is the ground being of everything that exists; it is the source of pure love. It has many names such as Presence, Silence, Being, Existence to name a few.

Absolute Reality—Pure Consciousness or the transcendental reality beyond the time, space and causation; the objective of yoga

Awareness—witnessing or knowing aspect of Being

Being—the unchanging, Pure Consciousness which is the substratum of all phenomena; the eternal aspect of all beings

Bhakti—pure love, devotion, expressed generally towards the one aspect of the Divine

Bliss—our true nature experienced in the complete absence of thoughts

Cosmic Mother—Nature

Creation—includes all forms of creation such as physical, astral (mind) and causal (the cause of the previous two)

Creator—Pure Consciousness in association with its creative aspect or energy; God

Dharma—the eternal laws behind the Creation; the inherent nature of something; the laws that sustain the existence of anything in the Creation

Divine—see Supreme

Eternal Being—see Being

Existence—the Absolute Existence or Being as to differentiate it from the relative or limited existence within the form and name, or body and mind. The relative existence is limited and defined by time and space, whereas the Absolute Existence is beyond the time and space; it never comes into being and never ceases to exist

Heart of the Divine—Pure Consciousness

Infinite Love— one of the characteristics of Pure Consciousness, Existence or Being

Infinite Existence—Pure Consciousness or the Absolute Reality beyond the concept of space

Infinite Reality—Pure Consciousness or the Absolute Reality beyond the concept of time

Ishwara Consciousness—cosmic consciousness

Karma—Law of cause and effect which governs all life

Kundalini Shakti—the Infinite Energy of the whole Creation existing in a potential form in ordinary human beings but fully awakened in Realized Beings

Light—Pure Consciousness as self-revealing consciousness

Now—the Eternal nature of Pure Consciousness, beyond the time as such

Oneness—the experience of Pure Consciousness as existing in all

One Reality—the level of Pure Consciousness that is the reality behind everything

Pure Consciousness—The substratum of all other forms of consciousness and mental states. The ground consciousness behind the wakeful state, dream state, and the deep sleep state. It is an unmodulated awareness that remains the same even in the absence of objects. It is pure Existence.

Reality—see Absolute Reality

Samadhi—Superconscious state

Self—Pure Consciousness, see Being

Self-realization—the realization of the Absolute Reality behind all phenomena, enlightenment

Soul—Consciousness associated with the mind

Spirit—Awareness within associated with the mind; see Soul

Supreme—the (Divine) or Supreme Consciousness that permeates the whole Creation

Supreme Love—unconditional love that knows no differentiation of any kind. It is pure, cosmic experience and the very nature of us as Pure Consciousness.

Ultimate Nature—Pure Consciousness

Unifying Principle—the laws behind the Creation; the laws that sustain everything in balance; also called Dharma

Union—in the spiritual sense this means the Union on the level of Pure Consciousness. In the ultimate sense all separation is illusory and the Union is the reality; Union between the individual consciousness or Soul with the Cosmic consciousness or Soul.

Viveka—discrimination between the Pure Consciousness as a substratum Reality and phenomena